The making of Don't Die

Fans' Unofficial Guide to Unpack Bryan Johnson's Quest for Eternal Life

Jimmie B. Wald

Copyright page

All rights reserved. No part of this publication may be reproduced, distributed, or transmitted in any form or by any means, including photocopying, recording, or other electronic or mechanical methods, without the prior written permission of the publisher, except in the case of brief quotations embodied in critical reviews and certain other noncommercial uses permitted by copyright law.

Copyright © 2025, Jimmie B. Wald

Disclaimer Page

This book examines and analyzes the Netflix documentary Don't Die: The Man Who Wants to Live Forever, which follows Bryan Johnson's quest for immortality and anti-aging. This book's views, interpretations, and conclusions are entirely the author's own and may not represent the opinions, perspectives, or support of any person or group connected to Bryan Johnson, the documentary, or any of the organizations listed.

This book is meant solely for informational and recreational purposes and is not an official guide. Although every attempt has been made to assure the correctness of the information provided, no assurances are given as to the reliability of the scientific theories, medical assertions, or private practices included. Before making any decisions pertaining to their own health, readers are advised to use caution while implementing any of the wellness or health practices discussed and to get advice from a qualified healthcare provider.

Any acts based on the material in this book are not subject to the author's liability or accountability. Unless otherwise noted, any likeness to actual people—living or dead—is entirely coincidental.

Table of content

Copyright page 2

Disclaimer Page 3

Chapter one 7
    Meet Bryan Johnson 7

Chapter two 14
    The Quest for Immortality 14

Chapter three 25
    Family Dynamics 25

Chapter four 34
    Science versus Pseudoscience 34

Chapter five 46
    The Public Persona 46

Chapter six 64
    Cultural and Ethical Implications 64

Chapter seven 76
    Chris Smith's Directorial Vision 76

Chapter eight..84
  Critical Reception..84

Chapter nine...93
  The Future of Longevity..93

Conclusion... 98

Chapter one

Meet Bryan Johnson

The mysterious character at the center of the provocative documentary "Don't Die: The Man Who Wants to Live Forever," Bryan Johnson, has had an incredible journey that has made him a biohacking pioneer and a tech entrepreneur. Johnson's early life was influenced by the principles and teachings of his religion because he was born and reared in a Mormon household. But as he became older, he started to doubt Mormon doctrine and ultimately decided to quit the church, which would have a significant effect on his family relationships.

Johnson's business zeal and sharp mind carried him onward in spite of this emotional turmoil. After joining the tech sector, he immediately established himself as a trailblazer and innovator. Johnson's early business endeavors were centered on creating innovative payment apps, which he later sold and made a fortune from. He was able to follow his genuine passion—the desire to live a long life and to stop the aging process—because of his financial success.

Being a software entrepreneur, Johnson had always been captivated by how technology could improve and change people's lives. He believed that the quick developments in domains like data science, biotechnology, and artificial intelligence may be used as instruments to discover the causes of aging and possibly increase human longevity. As a result of his riches and experience, Johnson decided to push the boundaries of human optimization.

Johnson started his adventure into the realm of biohacking with the straightforward yet revolutionary notion that the human body is a complicated system that can be improved and maximized by combining technology, science, and self-discipline. He threw himself into longevity research, speaking with top authorities and investigating innovative cures and treatments that could slow down or even reverse the aging process.

Johnson created "Blueprint," a thorough health regimen that would serve as the foundation for his pursuit of immortality during this rigorous time of research and experimentation. Blueprint is a painstakingly planned regimen that covers every facet of Johnson's everyday existence, from his diet and breathing to his exercise routine and medical procedures.

Johnson created a series of algorithms at the core of Blueprint to maximize his body's capabilities. Regardless of his conscious wants or appetites, these algorithms are made to provide his body precisely what it needs, when it needs it. Johnson thinks he can retain the physical appearance of someone considerably younger than his actual age by living according to these rules.

Johnson has put together a group of medical professionals, researchers, and technicians to carry out Blueprint, and they are constantly keeping an eye on his biometric data. Every day, he goes through a litany of tests and treatments, including imaging scans, blood work, and experimental treatments, including gene therapy and plasma exchanges. In addition, he maintains a hard exercise routine that challenges his body to its limits and a tight diet that is customized to meet his specific nutritional demands.

Although others might consider Johnson's strategy radical or even obsessive, he sees it as an essential step in his fight against aging and for achieving optimum health. He thinks that by putting himself through this rigorous degree of self-monitoring and optimization, he is creating the foundation for a time when people will be able to take charge of their own biology and live far longer than is currently feasible.

The underlying conviction that aging is a sickness that may be treated and possibly healed rather than an inexorable process lies at the heart of Johnson's purpose. According to him, the human body is a machine that can be tweaked and kept in top condition for far longer than the average person's lifetime. He has questioned many of the presumptions and norms around aging and mortality as a result of this viewpoint.

Johnson contends that rather than being a scientific truth, our cultural conditioning has led us to embrace aging and death as normal and inevitable. He thinks that we may overcome these constricting ideas and realize the full potential of the human species by embracing the instruments and technology of the contemporary day. According to Johnson, aiming for longevity is a moral requirement that has the capacity to lessen suffering and improve humankind, not merely a personal goal.

Johnson's theory is not without its skeptics and critics, though. Since the long-term ramifications of his experimental treatments are unknown, several medical experts consider his technique to be unproven and perhaps harmful. Others wonder about the moral ramifications of people going to such lengths to prolong their lives and the possible social repercussions of living in a society where death is no longer a given.

Johnson is still pursuing immortality in spite of these objections. He views his purpose as a trailblazing attempt to push the envelope of what is conceivable and to encourage others to follow in his footsteps while he battles death. He wants to start a larger discussion about the future of human lifespan and how technology and personal agency will influence it by setting an example and advocating for change.

Johnson acknowledges that his path is quite personal and is motivated by his own aspirations and anxieties. He admits that his obsession with staying healthy has negatively impacted his connections with his family, especially with his son Talmage, who is about to go to college. Despite these difficulties, Johnson is steadfast in his belief that death and aging are not unavoidable in the future.

In the end, Bryan Johnson's tale is one of unbridled ambition, unwavering willpower, and a readiness to push the envelope in the service of human progress. His thoughts and deeds have undoubtedly influenced the discussion of longevity and the destiny of the human species, regardless of whether he is seen as a visionary pioneer or a misguided zealot. Johnson's pursuit of immortality is a complicated and contentious one, but it is also a profoundly human tale of one man's wish to rise above the confines of his own mortality, as the documentary "Don't Die" demonstrates.

Chapter two

The Quest for Immortality

Bryan Johnson's carefully planned daily schedule, which incorporates every element of his life, is the cornerstone of his search for longevity. His "Blueprint," as he refers to it, is a complete health regimen designed to slow down the aging process and maximize his body's function. Johnson has an almost obsessive level of discipline and precision when it comes to his nutrition, sleep, and exercise regimen, but he feels that this level of control is required to fulfill his dream of eternal life.

Johnson's food is an important part of his daily regimen. He adheres to a rigorous dietary regimen that is customized to meet his unique nutritional requirements and intended to give his body the best possible balance of nutrients. Johnson's diet is founded on the ideas of intermittent fasting and calorie restriction, which have been demonstrated in animal experiments to have potential longevity advantages. With an emphasis on whole, unadulterated foods that are high in vitamins and minerals, he eats a carefully balanced combination of proteins, fats, and carbohydrates.

Johnson uses cutting-edge technology to monitor every part of his diet to make sure he is getting the appropriate nutrients in the proper proportions. He can adjust his food intake according to his body's reaction because he wears a continuous glucose monitor that continuously analyzes his blood sugar levels. In order to track his nutrient levels and modify his diet appropriately, he also regularly has blood tests and other diagnostic procedures performed.

Johnson considers sleep to be an essential part of his longevity program, in addition to his food. He understands that the body needs sleep for its regeneration and repair processes and that long-term sleep deprivation can have a number of detrimental health repercussions. Johnson adheres to a rigorous routine to maximize his sleep, which enables him to have a steady quantity of restful sleep every night.

Johnson's sleep regimen starts with a meticulously regulated setting intended to encourage rest and reduce disturbances. He sleeps without being exposed to artificial light in a room that is kept at a cool temperature and is totally dark. He also employs cutting-edge technology, such as a brain wave tracking gadget and a smart mattress that adapts to the temperature and motion of his body, to keep an eye on his sleep patterns and quality.

Before going to bed, Johnson uses a variety of relaxation methods, including deep breathing exercises and meditation, to improve his quality of sleep. In the hours before bed, he also stays away from stimulating activities like watching TV or using electronics because the blue light they create might disrupt the body's normal sleep-wake cycle.

Another important part of Johnson's daily routine is exercise, which he approaches with the same amount of focus and discipline as his sleep and food. Johnson maintains a strict exercise routine that is intended to increase cardiovascular health and lifespan as well as strength, endurance, and flexibility.

High-intensity interval training (HIIT), strength training, and endurance exercises are all a part of Johnson's fitness regimen. He usually spends many hours a day exercising, targeting various muscle groups and energy systems with a range of tools and methods. Johnson uses cutting-edge technology, including a heart rate monitor and a device that counts his oxygen use and calorie burn, to track his performance during each workout.

Johnson also includes a variety of recuperation and regeneration procedures in his daily routine to optimize the lifetime advantages of his fitness regimen. These include procedures like infrared sauna therapy, which employs heat to encourage circulation and purification, and cryotherapy, which exposes the body to extremely low temperatures in an effort to reduce inflammation and improve healing.

Johnson feels that this degree of control and discipline is required to reach his goal of living forever, even though his approach to diet, sleep, and exercise may seem severe to some. He intends to slow down the aging process and sustain optimal physical and cognitive function well into his senior years by making the most of every part of his daily routine. It is unclear if this strategy will ultimately be effective, but Johnson's unwavering devotion to his pursuit of immortality is impossible to ignore.

Along with his demanding daily schedule, Bryan Johnson is investigating a variety of experimental cures and treatments that he thinks could be the secret to extending human life. These therapies, which are frequently at the forefront of medical research, aim to address the biological mechanisms that underlie aging and illness.

Plasma exchange, which substitutes a younger donor's blood plasma for some of Johnson's, is one of the most contentious procedures he has had.

The premise behind this treatment is that young people's blood contains substances that can aid in the regeneration and rejuvenation of aging tissues and organs. Despite some encouraging findings in animal research, plasma exchange's efficacy in humans is still mostly unclear, and many specialists advise against using it without more investigation.

Johnson has accepted plasma exchange as a possible strategy in his pursuit of longevity, even in the absence of solid proof. Using plasma provided by his teenage son, he has received several treatments and reports a variety of advantages, such as more energy, better sleep, and a quicker recovery from physical activity. Critics counter that any possible advantages of plasma exchange are outweighed by the hazards, which can include infections, allergic reactions, and other issues.

Gene therapy, which modifies the body's genetic material to treat or prevent disease, is another experimental medicine that Johnson is researching. Numerous age-related illnesses, including cancer, heart disease, Alzheimer's, and Parkinson's, may be targeted by gene therapy. Although it is still in its infancy, gene therapy has demonstrated promise in the treatment of some hereditary illnesses, and scientists are looking at how it might be used to extend life.

Johnson has received gene therapy treatments in nations like Honduras, where laws governing these operations are less strict. He thinks he can slow down or perhaps reverse the molecular processes that lead to these illnesses by focusing on particular genes linked to aging and disease. Gene therapy is still a very experimental and contentious topic, though, and many experts advise against using it without more study and regulatory control.

Johnson is investigating a variety of additional experimental treatments and therapies in addition to gene therapy and plasma exchange. These include nanomedicine, which employs microscopic particles to carry medications and other therapeutic agents straight to the cells and organs where they are required, and stem cell treatment, which uses stem cells to repair damaged or diseased tissues.

Johnson thinks that these treatments are the secret to extending human lifespan and realizing his dream of eternal life, even if they are still mainly unproven. In order to achieve this aim, he is prepared to assume the risks and uncertainties that come with these experimental medicines. He also hopes that his experiences will contribute to the advancement of longevity research and open the door for future discoveries.

Bryan Johnson's pursuit of immortality is heavily reliant on technology, and he is using a variety of state-of-the-art instruments and platforms to track his health, enhance his performance, and learn more about the aging process. Johnson is utilizing technology to control his body and mind in a way that has never been possible before, from wearables that monitor his biometric data to sophisticated AI algorithms that examine his health trends.

Monitoring his biometric data is one of the main ways Johnson is utilizing technology to assist his longevity strategy. His heart rate, blood pressure, oxygen levels, and brain activity are just a few of the physiological characteristics that are monitored by the several sensors and gadgets he wears. These gadgets give him up-to-date information on how well his body is functioning, enabling him to modify his sleep, exercise, and food regimens as necessary.

Johnson receives wearable technology in addition to routine diagnostic examinations and treatments that give a more complete picture of his health. These include blood testing, genetic analysis, and sophisticated imaging methods like MRI and CT scans that can detect possible health problems and direct focused interventions.

Johnson uses cutting-edge AI algorithms and machine learning techniques to interpret all of this data. By analyzing enormous volumes of data from various sources, these systems are able to spot trends and connections that human observers would overlook. Johnson's AI platform can offer a thorough picture of his health status and offer tailored suggestions for maximizing his performance by combining data from his wearable technology, diagnostic testing, and other sources.

In addition to keeping an eye on his personal health, Johnson is using AI to learn more about longevity studies in general. He created a platform called OS Fund that finds promising entrepreneurs and longevity research initiatives using machine learning techniques. The OS Fund can assist in determining the most promising areas for investment and encourage the development of innovative technologies and medicines by examining financing, publication, and other metrics data.

But Johnson uses technology for more than just tracking and analysis. Additionally, he is investigating how artificial intelligence (AI) and other cutting-edge technology might directly affect the aging process. He has, for instance, made investments in businesses creating AI-driven drug discovery systems that can find novel substances and treatments with potential anti-aging effects. The ability of AI to create individualized treatment programs based on each patient's own genetic and physiological profile also piques his attention.

In the end, Johnson thinks that technology will be essential to realizing his wish to live forever. He aims to better understand the biological mechanisms that lead to aging and create focused therapies that can halt or even reverse these processes by utilizing data, artificial intelligence, and other cutting-edge technologies. Johnson is dedicated to pushing the limits of what is feasible in pursuit of this vision, even though the route to immortality is still unclear. He is positive that technology will play a significant role in enabling this audacious aim.

Chapter three

Family Dynamics

In the documentary "Don't Die: The Man Who Wants to Live Forever," Bryan Johnson's interactions with his family—especially his son Talmage—take center stage amid his unrelenting quest for life and his unorthodox approach to health and wellbeing. Meanwhile, Johnson struggles with parenting and the effects of his choices on his family while pursuing immortality.

As Johnson's closest child, Talmage is a senior in high school who is about to undergo a significant life change. According to the documentary, their connection is characterized by both intense love and the inevitable conflicts that occur when a parent's compulsive pursuit of one objective threatens to eclipse their child's wants and desires.

Johnson casually mentions to Talmage that he intends to take 130 tablets in a single day, revealing to him the scope of his daily supplement regimen. This is one of the most startling scenes in the movie. The pressure that Johnson's rigorous attitude to health exerts on their relationship is evident from Talmage's worried and incredulous expression. It serves as a reminder that, despite his seemingly idealistic intentions, Johnson's decisions have practical repercussions for those closest to him.

The father-son relationship endures despite these difficulties. Talmage obviously loves and respects his father, even as he struggles with the changes that will come with moving away for college. For his part, Johnson understands the value of his relationship with his kid and the necessity of striking a balance between his personal interests and his parental duties.

The emotional toll that Johnson's search has on his family is not downplayed in the documentary. It is evident that his unwavering emphasis on lifespan has occasionally come at the price of other significant facets of his life. Johnson, however, is unable to deny the basic reality that relationships—especially those with our children—are what gives life meaning and purpose, even pushing the limits of human optimization.

Johnson must face the fact that, despite his best efforts to regulate his own biology, he cannot stop time or his son's life's natural course as Talmage is ready to leave home and go on his own adventure. It serves as a moving reminder that family ties and the experiences we have with our loved ones are what really make life worthwhile, especially for those who aspire to eternal life.

Bryan Johnson's use of plasma exchange therapy, which substitutes a younger donor's blood plasma for some of his own, is one of the most contentious and eye-catching elements of his longevity regimen. In a startling turn of events, the documentary discloses that Johnson's father, Richard, and his teenage son, Talmage, have also participated in similar therapies, fostering a peculiar and frightening kind of intergenerational relationship.

Plasma exchange therapy is based on the theory that younger people's blood contains substances that can aid in the regeneration and rejuvenation of older tissues and organs. Johnson has accepted the treatment as a possible instrument in his pursuit of longevity, despite the fact that there is little scientific support for this assertion and that it is unknown what the treatment's long-term effects will be.

Numerous moral and psychological issues are brought up by the choice to include his father and son in this experimental treatment. On one level, it might be interpreted as a potent representation of the generational sharing of lifeblood and the unshakable ties of family. The concept of a father and son uniting in this way, joined together by a shared desire to support one another and push the limits of what is possible, is unquestionably moving.

However, the documentary does not downplay the arrangement's disturbing ramifications. Many people find it quite disturbing that a parent would use their child's blood to try to prolong their own life; it conjures up thoughts of exploitation and vampires. It serves as a clear reminder of the extent some people would go to in order to achieve their objectives, even if doing so means stepping over boundaries that others might find unimaginable.

It is impossible to overlook the psychological effects of this type of intergenerational bonding, even outside the ethical issues. Talmage must have felt tremendous pressure to back his father's pursuit of immortality, even if it meant sharing his own bodily fluids. No child should have to carry this load, which may have long-term consequences for their emotional health and sense of independence.

The documentary emphasizes the awkward dynamics at work by presenting the plasma exchange moments in an uneasy manner. It is a potent and unnerving vision to see Johnson, his kid, and his father lying side by side with their blood dripping between them. It serves as a reminder that even when pursuing admirable objectives, there are boundaries and lines that must be respected for the sake of our own humanity and the welfare of people we care about.

As the documentary tells Bryan Johnson's biography, it becomes evident that his pursuit of longevity and his unorthodox approach to wellness and health did not develop overnight. Instead, they come from his personal struggles to balance family and faith.

Johnson's decision to quit the Mormon Church, which had a huge impact on his relationships with his loved ones, was one of the most important turning points in his life. Being raised in a pious Mormon household, Johnson's identity and sense of place were closely linked to his religious beliefs. In addition to giving up a set of values and customs that had influenced his life, leaving the church also put him at risk of losing the acceptance and support of his family and community.

The emotional toll that this choice placed on Johnson and his family is discussed in the documentary, along with hints of the complicated relationships and conflicts that developed as a result. It is evident that this decision caused tension in Johnson's relationship with his father in particular, as the senior Johnson found it difficult to reconcile his own strong religious beliefs with his son's decision to leave.

According to Johnson, his decision to leave the church was more than just a question of taste or opinion. But it was a deep look at his life's foundations. Johnson was rejecting a set of principles and presumptions that had governed his family for many generations when he disapproved of the church's doctrine and authority.

It is possible to view this departure from custom and the ensuing family strife as a microcosm of the more significant difficulties Johnson would later encounter in his quest for longevity. As he pushed the limits of conventional thinking in his desire to live forever, he would encounter criticism and suspicion from the medical establishment and the general public, just as he had to deal with the opposition and disbelief of his loved ones when he left the church.

Johnson was unable to resist the pull of family and the innate need for connection and belonging while forging his own route and adopting a drastically different set of values and customs. For instance, his choice to include his father and son in his plasma exchange treatment may be interpreted as an effort to reconcile his history and present and to find a means of preserving family ties while pursuing a future that many would find unthinkable.

Johnson's tale goes beyond immortality and cutting-edge longevity science. It is also a profoundly human tale of the difficulties and sacrifices involved in paving one's own way, as well as the anguish and delight of negotiating the complexities of faith and family. In order to create a life that is not just longer but also richer and more meaningful, Johnson must find a way to balance his unique vision with the wants and wishes of those closest to him while pushing the limits of human optimization.

Chapter four

Science versus Pseudoscience

Following internet entrepreneur Bryan Johnson's drastic attempts to slow down the aging process, the documentary "Don't Die: The Man Who Wants to Live Forever" explores the contentious field of biohacking. Johnson's pursuit of longevity challenges accepted medical wisdom, but it also calls into question the viability of his strategy from a scientific standpoint as well as the advantages and disadvantages of biohacking.

Numerous professionals comment on Johnson's strategies throughout the movie, providing analysis of the possible benefits and disadvantages of his outlandish tactics. Certain elements of Johnson's regimen, like his emphasis on diet, exercise, and sleep, are recognized by some experts as being based on accepted scientific theories. It has been demonstrated that these essential components of a healthy lifestyle enhance general well-being and may even lengthen life expectancy.

The more radical and experimental aspects of Johnson's strategy, such as his use of plasma exchange therapy and his gene therapy experiments, have drawn criticism from a number of academics. Although the future of longevity research may benefit from these innovative treatments, little is known about their long-term benefits and safety. Without appropriate medical supervision and scientific validation, experts warn that such treatments may have unforeseen outcomes and pose major health concerns.

The absence of a systematic, scientific approach in Johnson's biohacking activities is one of the main concerns brought up by specialists. It is practically impossible to identify which interventions are genuinely responsible for any apparent improvements when several treatments and therapies are combined at the same time. It is challenging to draw significant conclusions regarding the effectiveness of Johnson's methodology due to this lack of scientific rigor, which also calls into doubt the reproducibility of his findings.

Additionally, experts note that Johnson's reported benefits—such as increased energy and a quicker recovery from exercise—may be primarily due to the placebo effect. Even in the absence of scientifically validated interventions, the power of belief and expectancy can significantly influence a person's subjective perception of health and well-being. This event emphasizes how crucial it is to carry out thorough, controlled research in order to distinguish between real physiological impacts and psychological ones.

Some experts agree that Johnson's well-publicized biohacking attempts have contributed to a wider discussion about the direction of longevity research, notwithstanding these reservations. Johnson has raised awareness of the possibilities of new technology and treatments in the field of life extension by pushing the envelope of what is thought to be feasible and questioning conventional wisdom about aging. Even though his techniques are debatable, his enthusiasm and commitment have motivated others to consider the potential of human optimization and the pursuit of a longer, healthier life in greater detail.

In the end, the documentary's expert viewpoints emphasize how intricate and varied the fields of longevity research and biohacking are. Exploring non-traditional approaches to health and wellness may have advantages, but it is important to move cautiously and to put safety and scientific validity first. Finding a balance between creativity and accountability will be crucial as longevity science develops further, making sure that any breakthroughs are supported by thorough research and the highest ethical standards.

The medical world has harshly criticized Bryan Johnson's unconventional approach to biohacking and his pursuit of immortality, with many professionals voicing serious doubts about the safety and scientific validity of his techniques. The documentary "Don't Die: The Man Who Wants to

Live Forever" highlights the worries and objections expressed by medical professionals, showcasing some of these critical viewpoints.

Johnson is frequently criticized for his lack of scientific rigor and his reliance on anecdotal data rather than controlled, peer-reviewed investigations. Despite being eye-catching, many medical professionals and researchers contend that Johnson's self-experimentation does not provide conclusive scientific evidence of the efficacy of his treatments. They make the point that without adequate validation through randomized, controlled studies, individual experiences—no matter how compelling—cannot be extended to the larger community.

Dr. Vadim Gladyshev, a professor of medicine at Harvard who is interviewed in the documentary, offers a particularly scathing assessment of Johnson's methods. "It's not science," he asserts, dismissing Johnson's approach as mere attention-seeking rather than a genuine contribution to the field of longevity research.

Gladyshev's statement reflects a widespread sentiment among medical professionals that Johnson's biohacking endeavors are more about generating publicity than advancing scientific knowledge.

Another major point of contention is Johnson's willingness to engage in experimental treatments that have not been thoroughly tested for safety and efficacy. His use of plasma exchange therapy, for example, has been met with skepticism and concern from medical experts who warn that the long-term effects of such treatments are unknown. Similarly, his experimentation with gene therapy in Honduras has raised eyebrows among those who believe that such interventions should only be pursued under strict regulatory oversight and with a clear understanding of the potential risks involved.

Critics also argue that Johnson's approach, which involves combining multiple treatments and therapies simultaneously, makes it impossible to determine which interventions are actually responsible for any perceived benefits. This lack of scientific clarity is seen as a major flaw in his strategy, as it prevents the identification of specific mechanisms of action and hinders the development of targeted, evidence-based interventions for aging.

Furthermore, medical professionals express concern about the potential dangers of promoting unproven and potentially risky practices to the general public. They worry that Johnson's high-profile biohacking efforts could encourage others to pursue similar interventions without proper medical guidance, leading to unintended consequences and possibly serious health complications. The responsibility of public figures like Johnson to communicate the limitations and uncertainties of their approaches is seen as a crucial ethical consideration.

Despite these criticisms, some medical experts acknowledge that Johnson's unconventional methods have helped to spark a broader conversation about the future of longevity research. While they may disagree with his specific practices, they recognize that his passion and dedication have brought attention to the potential of emerging technologies and therapies in the field of life extension. However, they emphasize the need for rigorous scientific validation and a cautious, evidence-based approach to ensure that any advances in longevity science are safe, effective, and ethically sound.

At the heart of the controversy surrounding Bryan Johnson's biohacking endeavors lies the fundamental question of scientific validity. As the documentary showcases, there is a sharp divide between Johnson's claims of success and the skepticism expressed by many in the medical and scientific communities.

One of the primary issues raised by critics is the lack of controlled, peer-reviewed studies to support the effectiveness of Johnson's interventions. While he may experience subjective improvements in his health and well-being, the absence of rigorous scientific evidence makes it difficult to attribute these benefits to his specific practices. Anecdotal reports, no matter how compelling, cannot replace the gold standard of randomized, controlled trials in establishing the efficacy of medical interventions.

Moreover, Johnson's approach of combining multiple treatments and therapies simultaneously poses a significant challenge to scientific validity. By engaging in a wide range of interventions, from dietary changes and exercise regimens to experimental therapies like plasma exchange and gene therapy, it becomes nearly impossible to isolate the effects of individual components. This lack of scientific clarity hinders the identification of specific mechanisms of action and makes it difficult to draw meaningful conclusions about the effectiveness of his methods.

Critics also point out that many of the benefits Johnson claims to experience, such as improved energy levels and faster recovery from exercise, could be largely attributable to the placebo effect. The power of belief and expectation can have a profound impact on an individual's subjective experience of health and well-being, even in the absence of scientifically proven interventions. This phenomenon underscores the importance of conducting rigorous, controlled studies to separate genuine physiological effects from psychological ones.

Furthermore, the long-term safety and potential risks associated with Johnson's experimental practices remain largely unknown. While some of his interventions, such as a healthy diet and regular exercise, are generally accepted as beneficial, others, like plasma exchange therapy and gene therapy, have not been thoroughly tested for their long-term effects. Engaging in such practices without a clear understanding of the potential consequences raises serious ethical and scientific concerns.

Another issue that undermines the scientific validity of Johnson's approach is the lack of transparency and peer review. Many of his claims and practices are promoted through his personal website and social media channels, rather than being subject to the rigorous scrutiny of the scientific community. This lack of external validation and oversight makes it difficult to assess the credibility of his assertions and raises questions about the reproducibility of his results.

Despite these criticisms, Johnson and his supporters argue that his unconventional methods represent a pioneering approach to longevity research. They contend that traditional scientific paradigms may be too slow and conservative to keep pace with the rapid advancements in technology and our understanding of the aging process. By pushing the boundaries of what is considered possible and challenging conventional wisdom, they believe that Johnson is helping to accelerate the development of new interventions and therapies for life extension.

However, even those who are sympathetic to Johnson's goals emphasize the need for scientific rigor and caution. While innovation and outside-the-box thinking are essential for progress, they must be balanced with a commitment to evidence-based practices and the highest ethical standards. The pursuit of longevity, no matter how noble, cannot come at the expense of scientific integrity and the well-being of individuals.

As the field of longevity research continues to evolve, it will be crucial to strike a balance between the desire for breakthrough discoveries and the need for scientific validity. Only by subjecting new interventions and therapies to rigorous testing, peer review, and oversight can we ensure that any advances in life extension are safe, effective, and grounded in sound scientific principles. The story of Bryan Johnson and his quest for immortality serves as a cautionary tale, reminding us of the importance of approaching the frontiers of science with a mix of enthusiasm, skepticism, and unwavering commitment to the truth.

Chapter five

The Public Persona

In the video, Harvard medical scholar Dr. Vadim Gladyshev provides a particularly critical evaluation of Johnson's practices. He declares, "It's not science," rejecting Johnson's strategy as merely attention-grabbing rather than a sincere advancement in the study of longevity. Medical professionals generally believe that Johnson's biohacking activities are more about creating notoriety than furthering scientific understanding, which is reflected in Gladyshev's comments.

Johnson's readiness to participate in experimental treatments that have not been adequately evaluated for safety and effectiveness is another significant area of debate. Medical professionals, for instance, have expressed skepticism and alarm over his use of plasma exchange therapy, stating that the long-term implications of such treatments are unclear. His gene therapy experiments in

Honduras have also drawn criticism from individuals who think that such operations should only be carried out with close regulatory supervision and after the possible risks have been thoroughly understood.

Additionally, critics contend that Johnson's strategy, which combines several therapies and treatments at once, makes it impossible to identify which interventions are truly in charge of any apparent advantages. This lack of scientific clarity is viewed as a significant weakness in his approach since it makes it difficult to pinpoint precise mechanisms of action and to create evidence-based, focused aging therapies.

Medical experts often voice concerns about the possible risks of recommending untested and maybe dangerous techniques to the general public. They are concerned that Johnson's well-publicized biohacking activities would inspire others to try similar treatments without the right medical supervision, which could have unforeseen repercussions and perhaps cause major health issues. One important ethical aspect is that prominent individuals like Johnson are obligated to disclose the limitations and uncertainties of their methods.

Some medical professionals agree that Johnson's unorthodox approaches have contributed to a wider discussion about the direction of longevity research in spite of these objections. They acknowledge that his enthusiasm and commitment have raised awareness of the possibilities of new technology and treatments in the field of life extension, even though they may not agree with his particular methods. To guarantee that any advancements in longevity science are secure, efficient, and morally sound, they stress the necessity of thorough scientific validation and a cautious, evidence-based approach.

The basic issue of scientific validity is at the center of the debate about Bryan Johnson's biohacking activities. This documentary demonstrates the stark contrast between Johnson's assertions of achievement and the doubts voiced by numerous members of the scientific and medical sectors.

The absence of controlled, peer-reviewed research to back up the efficacy of Johnson's therapies is one of the main concerns brought up by detractors. His health and well-being may improve subjectively, but it is challenging to link these gains to his particular habits in the lack of solid scientific proof. No matter how convincing they may be, anecdotal tales cannot take the place of randomized, controlled studies as the gold standard for determining the effectiveness of medical interventions.

Furthermore, Johnson's strategy of integrating several therapies and treatments at once seriously undermines scientific validity. It is practically hard to separate the impacts of different components when a variety of interventions are used, ranging from dietary modifications and exercise routines to experimental medicines like gene therapy and plasma exchange. This lack of scientific clarity makes it challenging to pinpoint precise mechanisms of action and to draw insightful conclusions regarding the efficacy of his techniques.

Many of the advantages Johnson claims to have, like increased energy and quicker recovery from exercise, may also be primarily due to the placebo effect, according to critics. Even in the absence of scientifically validated interventions, the power of belief and expectancy can have a significant impact on a person's subjective perception of health and well-being. This event emphasizes how crucial it is to carry out thorough, controlled research in order to distinguish between real physiological impacts and psychological ones.

Additionally, nothing is known about the long-term safety and possible hazards connected to Johnson's experimental procedures. Some of his treatments, like a balanced diet and consistent exercise, are widely acknowledged to be helpful, but others, like gene therapy and plasma exchange therapy, have not had their long-term consequences fully investigated. There are significant ethical and scientific issues when such practices are carried out without a thorough awareness of the possible repercussions.

The absence of peer review and transparency in Johnson's methodology is another problem that calls into question its scientific legitimacy. Instead of being rigorously examined by the scientific community, a large number of his assertions and practices are promoted on his own website and social media accounts. The lack of outside validation and supervision makes it difficult to verify his claims and doubt his findings' reproducibility.

Johnson and his proponents contend that his unorthodox techniques constitute a groundbreaking approach to lifespan research in spite of these objections. They argue that conventional scientific paradigms might be overly conservative and slow to keep up with the speed at which technology is developing and with our growing knowledge of aging. They think Johnson is accelerating the development of new interventions and therapies for life extension by questioning the status quo and pushing the limits of what is thought to be feasible.

Even supporters of Johnson's objectives, meanwhile, stress the importance of scientific integrity and prudence. While creativity and unconventional thinking are necessary for advancement, they must be weighed against a dedication to the highest ethical standards and evidence-based procedures. No matter how admirable, the quest for longevity cannot come at the price of individual welfare and scientific integrity.

Finding a balance between the necessity for scientific validity and the desire for ground-breaking findings will be essential as longevity research develops. We can only be sure that any advancements in life extension are safe, effective, and based on valid scientific principles by putting new interventions and therapies through rigorous testing, peer review, and oversight. We are reminded of the value of approaching the frontiers of science with a combination of enthusiasm, skepticism, and an uncompromising devotion to the truth by Bryan Johnson's story and his search for immortality.

The Netflix documentary "Don't Die: The Man Who Wants to Live Forever," which focused on software entrepreneur Bryan Johnson, caused a media frenzy in January 2023. His unorthodox approach to biohacking and his pursuit of immortality grabbed international attention, propelling him into the spotlight and igniting a heated discussion regarding the risks and benefits of his techniques.

Johnson's drastic efforts to slow down aging and possibly achieve eternal youth were the subject of the viral moment that catapulted him into the public eye. His rigorous daily routine, which included taking a combination of vitamins and minerals, keeping an eye on his body's processes using a variety of gadgets, and even testing out controversial therapies including blood transfusions from his teenage son, was covered by the media.

Johnson was an unavoidable topic for reporters and pundits due to the dramatic nature of his story and his position as a successful software tycoon. Some described him as a trailblazing innovator who was expanding the potential of the field of human optimization. They were astounded by his commitment to his objective and his readiness to put himself through such a demanding and unusual way of living in an effort to live a long life.

Others, however, adopted a more critical position, portraying Johnson as a quirky individual whose methods verged on fanaticism. They expressed worries about the possible dangers and moral ramifications of his experiments as well as the scientific validity of his procedures. Some even went so far as to call him a "vampire billionaire," squandering his own son's youth in an attempt to evade death.

Johnson's viral moment undoubtedly succeeded in grabbing the public's attention and igniting a larger discussion about the direction of longevity research, despite the conflicting responses. His tale appealed to people's enduring interest in the concepts of immortality and the ability of technology to improve humankind. It also emphasized the growing popularity of biohacking and people's desire to control their own health and well-being.

Johnson was in the center of a tornado of attention as the media coverage grew more intense. He was hailed as a representative of the state of the art in longevity science, asked to speak at conferences, and sought out for interviews. Others viewed him as a trailblazer who was pushing the envelope of what was conceivable and encouraging others to follow in his footsteps, while others wrote him off as a simple attention-seeker.

Ultimately, Bryan Johnson's viral moment was a potent reminder of how fascinated people have always been by the notion of perpetual youth and how far some people will go to achieve it. It also emphasized how complicated and frequently contentious the discussion of longevity research is, as well as how privilege and wealth can influence the course of scientific investigation. Johnson's story will probably continue to be a topic of discussion regarding the future of aging and the pursuit of immortality as it develops.

Following his viral moment, Bryan Johnson's public profile increased, and he started using his newfound notoriety to advertise his own health program, which he called the "Blueprint." Johnson tried to take advantage of the tremendous interest in his techniques and position himself as a prominent figure in the fields of longevity research and biohacking by launching a clever marketing strategy that included everything from branded olive oil to nutritional supplements.

Johnson's line of dietary supplements, which he said were vital to his daily routine and his pursuit of optimal health, was at the center of his marketing campaigns. These supplements, which featured a precisely balanced combination of vitamins, minerals, and other nutrients, were marketed as the cornerstone of his Blueprint regimen and sold on his own website as well as other internet merchants.

The sleek, simple containers used to package Johnson's supplements gave off an air of cutting-edge technology and scientific accuracy. Each product's distinct formulation, as well as the stringent testing and quality control procedures that went into their creation, were highlighted by the branding. Johnson aimed to appeal to a burgeoning market of health-conscious consumers who were ready to take charge of their own well-being by presenting his supplements as the path to discovering the secrets of longevity.

Johnson expanded into the realm of branded food items in addition to his supplement line, most notably with the introduction of his own olive oil. Johnson's olive oil was promoted as a key part of his Blueprint diet and a way to support longevity and excellent cardiovascular health. It was hailed as a superior source of antioxidants and healthy fats.

Johnson's olive oil's branding was thoughtfully designed to convey an air of exclusivity and elegance. The sleek, dark bottles had simple labels that highlighted the superiority and special qualities of the oil. The marketing brochures made extensive use of Johnson himself, whose image was used to demonstrate the transformational potential of his Blueprint methodology.

Johnson used his substantial social media following and his regular media appearances to better market his goods and his broader concept of health and longevity. He frequently provided information on his daily activities, his most recent biometric readings, and his predictions for the direction of longevity studies. He also had direct conversations with his followers, responding to their inquiries and giving them tips on how to improve their own health and well-being.

However, Johnson's marketing activities were quickly criticized for having potential conflicts of interest. He was accused by some of exploiting his public position to endorse goods that had not undergone stringent regulatory scrutiny or scientific testing. Some questioned whether his emphasis on branded food items and supplements was more about making money than furthering longevity studies.

Notwithstanding these objections, Johnson's marketing approach was unquestionably successful in increasing his public reputation and sparking interest in his Blueprint plan. Johnson was able to reach a sizable consumer base of people who were keen to take charge of their own health by establishing himself as a pioneer in the fields of biohacking and longevity research and by providing a line of goods that claimed to help people reach their best health and possibly live longer.

The introduction of Bryan Johnson's "Rejuvenation Olympics" website was arguably the most notable example of his increasing impact in the fields of biohacking and longevity research. Described by Johnson as a "new sport and a new way to understand reality," this groundbreaking platform was an audacious attempt to gamify the pursuit of longevity and to provide a competitive framework for tracking and comparing individual development.

A set of subscription-based testing kits that enabled competitors to gauge their own "speed of aging" and monitor their development over time formed the core of the Rejuvenation Olympics. These kits were intended to offer a thorough evaluation of a person's general health and longevity potential. They contained a variety of biomarkers and physiological indications.

Johnson aimed to capitalize on the competitive nature that motivates many athletes and fitness enthusiasts by measuring the aging process and developing a leaderboard that ranked participants according to their performance. He thought he might encourage others to reach new heights and adopt the kind of methodical, data-driven approach that had been the hallmark of his own practice by portraying the quest for longevity as a sport with obvious victors and losers.

A devoted following of biohackers, longevity enthusiasts, and health-conscious people from all around the world soon gathered at the Rejuvenation Olympics. On social media, participants enthusiastically posted their results, comparing their scores and rejoicing in their advancement up the scoreboard. Some even started planning neighborhood gatherings and contests, fostering a sense of belonging and solidarity around the common objective of maximizing health and prolonging life.

For Johnson, his approach to longevity research and biohacking was finally validated by the Rejuvenation Olympics. He claimed to have reached an unparalleled state of health and energy, with biomarkers comparable to those of top sportsmen who were decades his junior. He asserted that he had slowed his own "speed of aging" to a mere 0.64, which meant that his body aged by only seven and a half months for each year that went by.

Although Johnson led the leaderboard on his own platform at first, a few other competitors who had adopted his Blueprint regimen and pushed themselves to even higher levels soon overtook him. Johnson was not deterred by this development; rather, he saw it as evidence of the effectiveness of his strategy and the possibility that others could attain comparable outcomes with commitment and self-control.

However, detractors expressed worries about the possible risks of promoting severe biohacking and self-experimentation without the necessary medical oversight or scientific support. Some were concerned that the Rejuvenation Olympics' competitive atmosphere would encourage athletes to take unwarranted chances or put their immediate interests ahead of their long-term health and well-being.

The Rejuvenation Olympics gained steam in spite of these reservations, garnering media coverage and creating excitement within the longevity and biohacking communities. Johnson saw the platform as the pinnacle of his work to change the way we see aging and motivate people to take charge of their own well-being and longevity.

As the Rejuvenation Olympics developed and grew, it became evident that Johnson had capitalized on a strong desire shared by many people to push the limits of human ability and longevity. There is no doubting the influence his public image and marketing campaigns have had on the discussion of aging and the pursuit of immortality, regardless of whether his strategy turns out to be long-term viable or scientifically sound.

Chapter six

Cultural and Ethical Implications

The Netflix movie "Don't Die: The Man Who Wants to Live Forever," which chronicles Bryan Johnson's quest for immortality, has generated a contentious ethical discussion over the propriety of biohacking and the pursuit of longevity. A basic question at the center of this discussion is whether it is ethically acceptable for people to use such drastic measures to prolong their lives and what the possible repercussions would be for society at large.

Those who contend that aiming for longevity is a desirable and worthwhile objective are on one side of the argument. They maintain that the desire to live a longer, healthier life is a basic human motivation and that new opportunities for accomplishing this aim have been made possible by scientific and technological advancements. According to this viewpoint, those like Bryan Johnson who are prepared to push the limits of biohacking and longevity research are trailblazers, opening the door for a time when people will be able to overcome the constraints of age and illness.

Supporters of this viewpoint contend that increased health and a longer lifespan provide societal as well as personal advantages. As justifications for promoting and supporting research into longevity and biohacking, they cite the possibility of greater productivity, lower healthcare expenses, and an improved standard of living for both individuals and society. They also argue that people should have the freedom to choose how they want to improve their health and live longer, and pursuing longevity is a basic human right.

Those who voice grave moral and ethical objections to the consequences of biohacking and the pursuit of immortality are on the opposing side of the argument. They contend that the quest for extremely long lifespans is a foolish and even hazardous undertaking that might have profound effects on society at large.

The potential for biohacking and longevity research to worsen already-existing disparities and establish a new class divide based on access to life-extending technologies is one of the main issues brought up by detractors. They contend that the vast majority of people will be left behind since only the wealthy and privileged, like Bryan Johnson, can afford the cutting-edge medications and treatments that claim to prolong lifetime. They argue that this could result in a world where the wealthy and powerful live for centuries while the underprivileged and disenfranchised continue to die young and suffer from illness.

The possible effects of longer life spans on resources and the environment raise further ethical questions. A world where people regularly live for 150 years or more, according to critics, would put an unsustainable strain on food supplies, healthcare systems, and natural resources. The psychological and sociological ramifications of such a society are also brought up, as people might find it difficult to find meaning and purpose in lives that last for decades longer than what is currently seen as a normal lifetime.

Others contend that, from a philosophical and spiritual standpoint, the quest for immortality is essentially erroneous. They argue that a life well lived requires accepting mortality, and death is an integral element of the human experience. According to this viewpoint, trying to avoid death is a sign of arrogance and a rejection of the universe's inherent order, which can only result in misery and disappointment.

In the end, there are beneficial arguments on both sides of the complicated and nuanced moral controversy surrounding biohacking and longevity research. It will be critical for society to address these ethical issues and create a framework for weighing the possible advantages of longevity research against the risks and difficulties it presents as scientific and technological advancements continue to push the limits of what is feasible in terms of human lifespan and health.

The documentary which tells the narrative of Bryan Johnson's quest for immortality, has highlighted a variety of social viewpoints on aging and death. These viewpoints, which are influenced by philosophical, theological, and cultural traditions as well as scientific and technological advancements, show the various and frequently conflicting ways that people and communities deal with death and aging.

Death is considered a normal and unavoidable aspect of the human experience in many countries. According to this viewpoint, seeking immortality is frequently seen as a pointless and foolish attempt, and accepting mortality is seen as an essential part of living a life well-lived. This perspective stems from a variety of religious and cultural traditions that stress the value of living in balance with nature and the cyclical nature of existence. For instance, attaining enlightenment and inner peace is said to require accepting impermanence and embracing the present moment in many Eastern philosophical and spiritual traditions, including Buddhism and Hinduism. According to this viewpoint, the pursuit of perpetual life extension is a type of attachment and desire that can only result in misery and disillusionment.

Similar to this, death is frequently seen as a means of entering an afterlife and reuniting with the divine in many Western religious traditions, including Christianity and Islam. According to this viewpoint, the physical body is but a transient vehicle, and the emphasis is on leading a morally upright and purposeful life in order to prepare for the hereafter. In this perspective, the quest for immortality is frequently seen as a sign of arrogance and a rejection of the authority of a higher force.

Simultaneously, scientific and technological developments have questioned conventional wisdom regarding aging and mortality and have created new avenues for increasing human longevity and enhancing the quality of old age. For instance, the study of gerontology has advanced our knowledge of the biological processes behind aging and the creation of treatments to delay or even reverse it.

Some people believe that these developments portend a time when people will be able to live longer, healthier lives that are filled with more productivity. They contend that the goal of longevity is to maximize human lifespan potential and lessen the misery and incapacity brought on by age-related decline, not to avoid death.

Others, however, express worries about the effects that a longer lifespan and the quest for immortality will have on society. They contend that a society where people regularly live for centuries might have a number of unforeseen repercussions, ranging from resource depletion and overcrowding to the escalation of already-existing disparities and the breakdown of societal cohesiveness.

Some people also wonder if, from a psychological and emotional standpoint, pursuing immortality is indeed desirable. They contend that people can find significance and inspiration in accepting their mortality and realizing that life is limited, which inspires them to live it to the fullest and leave a positive legacy for coming generations.

The narrative of Bryan Johnson and his pursuit of immortality reflects complicated and nuanced social views on aging and death. It will be essential for people and communities to consider these issues and come up with a common understanding of what it means to live a healthy life in the face of mortality as scientific and technological advancements continue to push the limits of what is feasible in terms of human lifespan and health.

The film which tells the narrative of Bryan Johnson and his quest for immortality, poses a number of moral dilemmas about the pursuit of longevity and the effects of biohacking on both people and society at large. The allocation of resources, the escalation of inequality, the psychological and emotional effects of longer lifespans, and the possible hazards and unforeseen repercussions of experimental cures and technologies are only a few of the topics covered by these inquiries.

The problem of inequality and access is one of the main ethical issues brought up by Johnson's strategy. Being a successful software entrepreneur, Johnson has the means and contacts to seek innovative medicines and treatments that are unaffordable for the vast majority of people. If successful, the quest for extreme longevity, according to critics, could result in a future where the wealthy and powerful live for centuries while the underprivileged and disenfranchised continue to die young and suffer from illness.

This calls into question how funds for longevity research are allocated and how resources are distributed. Should resources be allocated to more urgent health and social concerns that impact the larger community, or should society prioritize the development of life-extending technology that would only benefit a small, privileged segment of the population?

The possible dangers and unforeseen repercussions of the experimental treatments and technologies that Johnson and other members of the biohacking community are investigating raise additional ethical questions. The long-term impacts of many of these interventions on human health and well-being have not been fully investigated, including gene therapy and the usage of unproven medications and supplements.

The quest for immortality at any cost, according to critics, may cause people to take needless chances and put their immediate interests ahead of their long-term well-being. Concerns are also raised regarding the possibility that these technologies will be abused or misused, either by people looking to obtain an unfair edge or by organizations and governments trying to manage and control populations.

The psychological and emotional effects of longer life spans on people and society at large raise ethical concerns as well. The quest for immortality, according to others, is a kind of avoidance and denial, a failure to face the facts of aging and death, which are an integral aspect of the human experience. They argue that people can find meaning and motivation in accepting their mortality and realizing that life is limited, which encourages them to make the most of their remaining time and develop closer relationships with others.

Others express worries that people may get bored and disconnected as a result of living longer than is currently thought to be normal because they will find it difficult to find meaning and purpose in lives that go on for decades or even centuries. They also wonder if a society where death is not a given would result in a deeper appreciation for life or in complacency and a disdain for the importance of every moment.

Lastly, there are moral concerns regarding the search for immortality's wider social ramifications and its capacity to drastically change the character of the human experience. The operation of human communities and the preservation of social cohesion, according to some, depend on the acceptance of mortality and the understanding of the cyclical nature of life and death. They argue that in a future where people frequently live for centuries, traditional family structures may disintegrate, intergenerational relationships may disappear, and the sense of common destiny and purpose that unites societies may erode.

Bryan Johnson's approach to biohacking and the quest for immortality raise intricate and nuanced ethical concerns that touch on matters of social cohesiveness, risk, access, and meaning. It will be essential for people and society at large to consider these issues and create a framework for weighing the possible advantages of longevity research against the dangers and difficulties it presents as scientific and technological developments continue to push the limits of what is feasible in terms of human lifespan and health.

Chapter seven

Chris Smith's Directorial Vision

Filmmaker Chris Smith, who is renowned for his ability to tell gripping stories about unusual people, adopted a methodical approach when making Don't Die: The Man Who Wants to Live Forever. Fundamentally, the documentary examines Bryan Johnson, a highly motivated but polarizing figure. Smith had to balance telling a gripping story with critically analyzing Johnson's biohacking mission without either supporting or discounting his dubious tactics.

Shortly after Johnson's viral headlines portrayed him as a "vampire billionaire tech bro," Smith started filming in March 2023. Smith gained insight into Johnson's mission's appeal and skepticism from this beginning point. In addition to chronicling Johnson's life, he aimed to reveal the facets of a man whose unrelenting quest for immortality pushes the boundaries of ethics, science, and social conventions.

Smith's focus on visual storytelling is one of his defining characteristics. The documentary juxtaposes order and obsession by alternating interviews with footage of Johnson's meticulously regimented daily life. Sharp, nearly antiseptic images that reflect Johnson's scheduled routine demonstrate the clinical precision of his life—waking up at the same time, eating the same precisely measured meals, and receiving experimental treatments. Personal moments, like his conversations with his adolescent son Talmage, are juxtaposed with these photos to give the story a more relatable touch.

Smith's choice to involve critics and scientific professionals emphasizes his impartial stance even more. Although Johnson frequently uses his own words to support his assertions, there are counterarguments from medical experts, including Harvard's Dr. Vadim Gladyshev, who criticize Johnson's approaches as "attention-seeking" rather than scientific. Smith lets viewers make their own judgments on Johnson's quest and the wider ramifications of biohacking by providing equal weight to both perspectives.

Smith also conducts interviews in a tactful yet direct manner. He discusses mortality, control, and the human condition in his talks with Johnson, delving into the reasons underlying his preoccupation with longevity. Instead of promoting a specific story, Smith's inquiries let Johnson be himself, warts and all.

Smith has previously documented the lives of ambitious people with wild ideas in Don't Die: The Man Who Wants to Live Forever. The quixotic voyage of Mark Borchardt, an independent director who was having difficulty finishing a low-budget horror picture, was chronicled in his 1999 film American Movie. The theme of both documentaries is the same: they examine the extent people would go to in order to achieve their goals, despite doubt and skepticism.

Borchardt's goals with American Movie were modest yet intensely personal. He was a sympathetic underdog because of his unwavering will to finish his movie in spite of emotional and financial obstacles. Bryan Johnson's mission in Don't Die, on the other hand, is far larger in scope, including millions of dollars, state-of-the-art technology, and a worldwide audience. However, the two main characters have a singular focus that verges on obsession.

Smith's portrayal of Borchardt was marked by a blend of empathy and humor, highlighting the ridiculousness of his hardships without lessening his fervor. However, the tone is more clinical in Don't Die, which reflects the complicated ethical issues and high stakes of Johnson's job. Johnson's struggles are internal, involving the human urge to overcome mortality itself, whereas Borchardt's mostly external problems were financial, temporal, and material.

The narrative rhythm of the two movies varies as well. Borchardt's struggles and victories serve as organic plot points as American Movie develops as a character-driven narrative. Conversely, Don't Die takes a more divided approach, alternating between Johnson's private life, research endeavors, and public image. This illustrates the complexity of Johnson's narrative, which touches on issues of ethics, technology, and interpersonal relationships.

Despite these variations, Smith's ability to see humanity in his subjects is a strength that unites the two movies. Whether capturing Johnson's painstakingly planned health regimen or Borchardt's tenacious resolve, Smith's ability to capture moments of vulnerability elevates his characters beyond mere representations of ambition.

Don't Die's ability to strike a balance between skepticism and empathy—a characteristic of Smith's filmmaking—is one of its distinguishing qualities. Given how divisive Bryan Johnson is, the documentary could have easily glorified his pursuit of immortality or reduced it to a warning about arrogance. Rather, Smith adopts a nuanced strategy that honors Johnson's journey's intricacy.

The inclusion of professional viewpoints and criticisms demonstrates the film's skepticism. Scientists and medical experts cast doubt on Johnson's methods, pointing out that his experiments lacked scientific rigor and that mixing experimental treatments has hazards. In order to prevent the movie from becoming an unquestioning platform for Johnson's beliefs, these voices act as a contrast to his assertions.

Smith also makes Johnson's humanity visible to the audience. His talks with Talmage, for example, show a father who is struggling with the same goals and anxieties as everyone else: the need to protect his loved ones, leave a legacy, and understand his role in the cosmos. These intimate interactions show the conflict between Johnson's emotional demands and his technological aspirations, standing in sharp contrast to the scientific detachment of his medical routine.

Smith also effectively conveys Johnson's character inconsistencies. Johnson talks fervently about how his techniques could help people, but his actions—from marketing his own brand of olive oil to selling supplements—frequently come out as self-serving. Johnson is shown in the movie as a flawed yet intriguing person, and these contradictions are not avoided.

Smith's inability to offer simple solutions is ultimately what allows him to strike a balance between skepticism and empathy. Though it leaves the spectator to consider these issues for themselves, the movie poses important queries regarding the morality of biohacking, the significance of mortality, and the boundaries of human ambition. Don't Die is a meditation on the human condition as a whole, not merely a documentary about one man's search for immortality, thanks to its flexible approach.

Smith crafts a picture that is both thought-provoking and emotionally impactful by fusing moments of sincere connection with critical critique. It pushes viewers to think about the wider ramifications of Johnson's search for a world that dares to defy death, in addition to the viability of his mission.

Chapter eight

Critical Reception

The movie release provoked a variety of responses from viewers, illustrating the intricacy and polarizing nature of the topic. The documentary received mixed reviews from viewers, with some applauding its provocative examination of aging and others denouncing it as a frivolous vanity effort. The movie's focus on Bryan Johnson, a successful businessman trying to avoid death, resonated with audiences who were curious about the morality and viability of biohacking.

Many people found the documentary to be an intriguing look at a future world where biology and technology coexist. Johnson's regimen and the wider ramifications of his quest became hot topics of discussion on social media sites like Reddit and Twitter. Some viewers praised Johnson as a pioneer in longevity science, and they praised his desire and discipline. Some others were optimistic about his efforts, as seen by remarks like, "He's not just living for himself; he's paving the way for the future of humanity."

But not everyone had such a favorable opinion of Johnson. His tactics were severe, and his manner was off-putting to many audience members. He was called a "tech bro caricature" by forum critics, who said he embodied the excesses of Silicon Valley. Others questioned the morality of his experiments, especially the contentious plasma transfusions that his adolescent son received. Some viewers were dubious of the documentary's purpose and the veracity of its subject since they believed the movie did not sufficiently refute Johnson's assertions.

Audiences frequently expressed a mixture of disgust and jealousy. Johnson maintained an amazing yet strange life of intense health monitoring. "Sure, he might live longer, but is that really living?" one viewer asked. Many questioned whether a longer life is worth the sacrifices Johnson promotes because of the contrast between his strict lifestyle and the satisfaction that comes from more impulsive, decadent activities, such as having a glass of wine or a late-night pizza.

The conflicting views of its audience were reflected in Don't Die's critical reception. Media sources debated the documentary's moral and cultural ramifications, frequently portraying it as a mirror of the fixation with youth and health in modern culture.

Good reviews emphasized the movie's capacity to provoke thought-provoking discussions about morality, science, and aging. The documentary was called "a timely exploration of humanity's oldest dream: to outwit death" by the New York Times. The review gave director Chris Smith credit for nuanced telling Johnson's story without completely supporting or refuting his assertions. The Guardian also praised the movie for taking a fair stance, pointing out that it showed both the advantages and disadvantages of Johnson's strategies.

However, unfavorable reviews faulted the documentary for showing too much sympathy for Johnson. Some critics believed that the movie gave him an unjustified platform to advocate for untested treatments by failing to challenge the pseudoscientific elements of his regimen. Rolling Stone called the documentary "a promotional piece masquerading as a documentary," while Variety claimed that it "skims the surface of Johnson's life without digging into the deeper questions his lifestyle raises."

Critics also pointed to Johnson's portrayal as a divisive character. Some media outlets regarded this as an effort to soften the image of a man who makes money from selling health products, while others valued the film's portrayal of his humanity, particularly in sequences involving his family. The Los Angeles Times questioned whether the use of Johnson's branded supplements and paraphernalia in the video made it difficult to distinguish between a commercial and a documentary.

The documentary's narrative and visual quality was one area where critics agreed. Smith's directing, which was widely praised for its compelling plot and crisp images, was praised. The Hollywood Reporter described the movie as "a visually arresting exploration of one man's obsessive quest," demonstrating that even critics recognized its technical merits.

Beyond its initial reaction, Don't Die has had a profound cultural impact, igniting discussions about aging, technology, and health in the future. The documentary has established itself as a benchmark for conversations about longevity research, biohacking, and the morality of aiming for immortality.

The movie's ability to popularize biohacking has been one of its most significant effects. Although the practice of enhancing the human body through technology and experimental treatments has long been marginalized, Don't Die brought it to the attention of a wider public. Because of this, phrases like "biological age" and "rejuvenation therapy" have become widely used, and many viewers are interested in finding out more about the science—or lack thereof—that is behind Johnson's techniques.

Discussions concerning fitness and healthcare accessibility have also been rekindled by the documentary. The inequality in who can afford to pursue such lofty health goals has been brought to light by Johnson's multimillion-dollar lifestyle, which is supported by his tech fortune. Although Johnson says his techniques could help humanity, critics have noted that they are currently exclusively available to a privileged elite. This has sparked more extensive conversations over the morality of creating therapies that put the lifespan of the individual ahead of the health equality of society.

The movie has solidified Johnson's status as a trailblazer and a contentious figure in the tech and wellness sectors. Since the release of the video, interest in his Blueprint program and website advertising the "Rejuvenation Olympics" has increased significantly. But this focus has also drawn criticism, with some doubting whether his commercial endeavors are motivated more by financial gain than by actual scientific advancement.

Don't Die has rekindled interest in the science of aging among academics. The movie has been utilized as a case study by academic institutions and research centers to examine the potential benefits and drawbacks of longevity science. Conferences and panels have been held to address the moral ramifications of biohacking, frequently using Johnson as a divisive example.

In terms of society, the documentary has made people reflect on their desire to live longer. Numerous viewers have shared that they have reexamined their own lifestyles, wondering if they put short-term pleasures ahead of long-term health. The movie has served as a wake-up call for some to change their unhealthy behaviors, while for others it has strengthened the conviction that life is only worthwhile when it is filled with brief moments of happiness.

Don't Die's influence on changing societal perceptions about death is arguably its most notable effect. The documentary challenges viewers' preconceived notions about aging and death by portraying Johnson's pursuit of immortality as both inspirational and concerning. It makes the audience consider how long and how they want to live in an age of rapid technological advancement—timeless and urgent questions.

Don't Die: The Man Who Wants to Live Forever is ultimately more than a documentary about a single man's infatuation with prolonging his life. It is a cultural relic that serves as a mirror to a society struggling with the benefits and risks of advancement, reflecting our shared fears and hopes. The movie has permanently changed the way we think about life, death, and the quest for something greater, regardless of whether it is seen as an uplifting story, a warning story, or a combination of the two.

Chapter nine

The Future of Longevity

In the future, according to tech entrepreneur Bryan Johnson, the protagonist of Don't Die: The Man Who Wants to Live Forever, aging will not be a natural occurrence but rather a problem that science can resolve. He refers to his grandiose ideology as "post-mortality," which seeks to redefine human life by escaping the limitations of biological aging. Johnson's program, dubbed the Blueprint, combines state-of-the-art technology, intense self-discipline, and experimental therapies in an effort to reduce aging at the cellular level.

Johnson's conviction that, with data-driven accuracy, people can manage and even reverse aging lies at the core of his vision. He has centered his life on algorithms that dictate every facet of his life, including his workout routine, food habits, sleep schedule, and even mental well-being. Johnson claims that by following this diet, he has considerably slowed down the aging process and is now physiologically decades younger than his 47-year-old chronological age.

Johnson's goal extends beyond self-improvement. He believes that aging is an antiquated constraint on human potential and imagines a time when artificial intelligence in particular will enable humanity to transcend death. His philosophy is extremely multidisciplinary, combining physics, biology, mathematics, and even ethics into one cohesive whole. According to him, "Don't Die is an ideology that crosses politics, economics, and spirituality; it's not just a health campaign."

But Johnson's theories present difficult issues. Is it possible for science to actually build an ageless world? If so, who stands to gain? Critics contend that these developments might exacerbate already-existing disparities and turn longevity into a luxury enjoyed only by the wealthy. Johnson, however, insists that his research has the potential to democratize health advancements, enabling everyone to live longer and healthier lives.

Johnson's vision of a post-mortality world is heavily reliant on developments in preventative medicine and health technology. Advances in biohacking, genetics, and artificial intelligence over the last ten years have completely altered our perspective on health. By emphasizing prevention and optimization, these advancements are changing the fundamentals of medicine and going beyond simple therapeutic instruments.

The application of AI to assess and improve human health is among the most exciting advancements in this area. These days, algorithms help identify illnesses before symptoms show up and offer personalized treatment recommendations based on each patient's unique genetic and biometric information. Johnson has gone one step further by developing gamified health tracking systems such as the Rejuvenation Olympics. Users can compete with others, track their biological age, and learn how to live as long as possible.

CRISPR and other gene editing technologies have the potential to be revolutionary as well. Scientists are opening the door to medicines that could greatly increase human lifespans by identifying and fixing genetic abnormalities connected to aging and disease. The limits of what is feasible in regenerative medicine are further explored by experimental therapies like the plasma transfusions, hyperbaric oxygen treatments, and sophisticated supplements that Johnson has embraced.

Additionally, preventative medicine is changing quickly, emphasizing lifestyle changes backed by evidence. This tendency is best illustrated by Johnson's Blueprint, which shows how exact control over sleep, exercise, and food may result in quantifiable health gains. Proponents contend that Johnson's trials push the limits of what science can accomplish and encourage a wider acceptance of preventative care measures, while detractors dispute the severe nature of his approaches.

The question of whether science can save the first generation is the most thought-provoking part of Johnson's proposal. Although this concept may seem like science fiction, it is becoming more and more plausible due to developments in longevity science. Johnson's research shows how combining the fields of bioengineering, genetics, and artificial intelligence (AI) can increase human lifespans and possibly even reverse aging.

Conclusion

Bryan Johnson's unrelenting quest for longevity and his vision for a post-mortality future are profoundly examined in the documentary Don't Die: The Man Who Wants to Live Forever. Fundamentally, the movie explores the relationship between science, ambition, and existential issues while highlighting humanity's always-changing relationship with age and mortality.

The fact that quickly developing technology is redefining the possibilities of human life is among the most important lessons learned. Viewers see how cutting-edge advancements in biohacking, artificial intelligence, and preventative medicine are used through Johnson's hyper-optimized regimen. Once the stuff of science fiction, these technologies are now a reality, although one that only a select few may use. Despite their controversy, Johnson's studies demonstrate how science has the power to disprove long-held beliefs about aging and pave the way for healthier, longer lives.

The documentary also highlights the shortcomings of today's healthcare systems, which frequently prioritize curing rather than preventing disease. When pursued to its utmost, Johnson's method—a careful balancing act of nutrition, exercise, sleep, and experimental therapies—showcases the effectiveness of preventative medicine. His lifestyle serves as a reminder of the value of preventive health management, even though most individuals won't follow his complete program.

However, the movie also highlights the moral and intellectual conundrums raised by the quest for immortality. Is eternal life for humans desirable or even possible? Who would benefit from a post-mortality world, and what would it look like? The documentary invites viewers to consider the wider ramifications of Johnson's search, leaving them with more questions than answers.

The part that personal agency plays in influencing our aging is one of the main topics of the documentary. Our everyday decisions—what we eat, how much exercise we get, and how we sleep—have an indisputable effect on our health and lifespan, even though genetic predispositions and environmental circumstances also play a part. Despite its extreme nature, Johnson's Blueprint is based on this idea.

Johnson's routine exemplifies the notion that gradual improvements can yield substantial outcomes. Even without access to cutting-edge technology or a team of experts, everyone can adopt the fundamental principles of eating nutrient-dense food, exercising frequently, and placing a high priority on restful sleep. His way of life stands in sharp contrast to the frequently harmful habits that many people form, such as unhealthy eating habits, sedentary lives, and long-term sleep deprivation.

But the movie also challenges the idea that aging can be resolved by personal decisions. Accessibility and equality are called into question by Johnson's reliance on costly therapies and an extensive support system. Is it feasible for the typical individual to implement even a small portion of his techniques? The documentary highlights structural obstacles that keep many individuals from putting their health first, such as cultural standards, lack of access to healthcare, and economic inequalities.

In the end, the movie makes the argument that although personal decisions are important, larger societal shifts must also be made. Health technology breakthroughs must become more widely accessible and reasonably priced if we are to make any real headway in prolonging healthy lifespans. Communities, healthcare institutions, and governments all have a part to play in fostering conditions that encourage extended life expectancy.

Myths, faiths, and innumerable scientific pursuits have all contributed to the age-old quest for immortality. Don't Die's portrayal of Bryan

Johnson's path is a contemporary version of this timeless pursuit. His narrative compels spectators to consider important issues like death, life, and what it means to be human.

Johnson's quest for immortality is unnerving as well as inspirational. His commitment to advancing science is, on the one hand, a testament to the greatest human desire and inventiveness. His faith in the potential for a brighter future is demonstrated by his readiness to test himself, to face criticism from the public, and to devote enormous financial resources to his pursuit. His art questions the present quo and provokes discussions about what is possible for humanity if we have the courage to have lofty dreams.

However, Johnson's trip presents moral questions. The concept of perpetual life extension has significant social ramifications. What effects might immortality have on global inequality, resource allocation, and population growth? Would it widen the gap between the rich and the poor that already exists? Furthermore, if death is no longer a given, what does it mean to live a meaningful life?

The video invites viewers to consider their own views on aging and mortality, but it makes no attempt to provide final answers to these concerns. Some people may find the prospect of eternal life alluring, while others may find it strange or even scary. The movie challenges viewers to consider these paradoxes, acknowledging that the pursuit of immortality is as much a philosophical as a scientific undertaking.

Don't Die ultimately serves as a reminder that pursuing immortality involves more than just extending one's life expectancy; it also entails improving the quality of those years. Johnson's story emphasizes the significance of living intentionally—of making decisions that are consistent with our values and goals—regardless of whether science succeeds in its goal of eradicating aging.

There is more to Don't Die: The Man Who Wants to Live Forever than just a documentary about a man's fight against aging. It is a contemplation on how people relate to time, health, and death. The film examines the potential and constraints of science, the strength of personal agency, and the important issues that come up when we doubt death's inevitability through Bryan Johnson's contentious and gripping tale.

The audience is left feeling both astonished and uneasy as the titles roll. Although Johnson's search may not yield all the solutions, it does give a window into a future in which life's limits are rethought. It remains to be seen if that future is desirable or achievable. For years to come, the pursuit of immortality will undoubtedly excite, provoke, and test us.

Printed in Dunstable, United Kingdom